Enchanted & Intoxicated Love

Words and Compilations of Amon Ra Nabmare

To order additional copies of this book, contact:
Xlibris
1-888-795-4274
www.Xlibris.com
Orders@Xlibris.com

Soul Mind

- *Incline Your ears to the sounds and tones of Soul Mind*

- *For Soul Mind is who I am*

- *I come to unfold my soul is after one goal*

- *I have to make sure my 3rd eye does not remain blind, in order for me to reach the Orion Skies*

- *For my mind is where I stay and there is where I unwind*

- *For my mind is where I stay to unfold all the lies form the synagogue*

- *I have to, it is imperative that my 3rd eye does not remain blind.*

- *There is a passion that grows within my Soul and Mind*

- *This passion is a direct blood link from my ancestors
  that flows within my Divine Soul*

- *For my ancestors have sent The One to show me how
  my mind, soul and aura supposed to glow green*

- *This passion within my soul and mind is a passionate desire of the unknown*

- *I must go back home and regain my crown and throne*

- *The unknown, I come to unfold my soul and mind is after one goal*

- *I have to make sure my 3rd eye remains clear in
  order for me to reach the Orion Skies*

- *Who am I, Soul Mind is who I am*

- *I will linger a craving that sparks your curiosity of the unknown*

- *The unknown is in our soul and mind*

- *For my mind is where I stay, there is where I unwind*

- *For my mind is where I stay to clear all the lies and fog from the synagogue*

- *Everything begins with the Creative Force, Source InnerG of The
  Multiverses, and from there it comes to our minds, our being*

- *For Soul Mind is who I am*

- *And with these two precious things I will return and
  regain my crown and throne back home*

- *Have no fear of the unknown*

Summer Breeze

- *Summer breeze, sweeter then molasses*

- *More beautiful than a golden leaf from the Tree of life*

- *Complexion like Carmel and a dash of Nutella*

- *Her skin hmmm... Like silky Silhouette*

- *Her eyes with a nice slant, that of a cat eyes*

- *Hey she maybe one of the Egyptian Goddess here in flash*

- *Eyes so deep, deeper than the deeper sea*

- *Non-penetrable as she is the one penetrating your soul*

- *Her stare will make you feel like she is swimming inside of you*

- *Now I believe that everything mother nature has made is perfect*

- *That's because she created you*

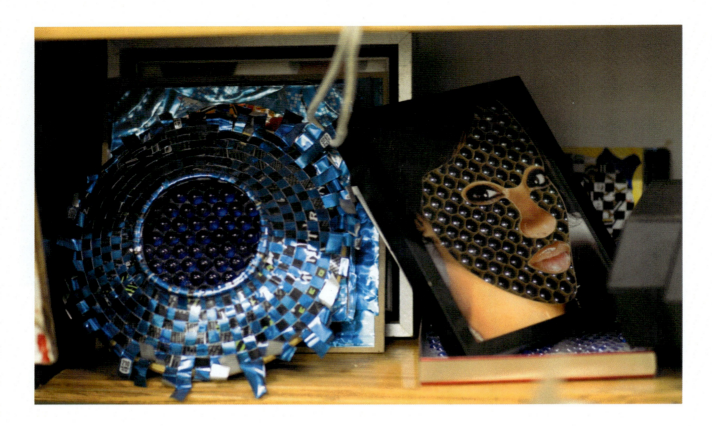

Mother Wise

- *How can I stop my mind from contemplating*

- *Contemplating about Mother of a Nation, Queen Goddess, Nubian Flower, Sweetness, Love-ness, Beauty-ness, Tender-ness, Mother Earth, Mother of the multiverse*

- *She has something I long for, something I can't live without*

- *I think about her 24-7 everyday*

- *And the reason is due to my desire for wisdom*

- *For it is only found next to her bosom*

- *When I wake from the cousin of death she is the first thing that comes to mind*

- *I stand on my feet, take a look out the window, and take a new breath of life*

- *I observe all the living things that has come to be*

- *It's positive forces that has come together to unite and ignite within the energy of the matter and the Atom of the unknown*

- *For the unknown are Her cells, Her nucleus, Her DNA*

- *For the unknown are Her cells, Her nucleus, Her DNA, Her RNA, Her Electromagnetic waves*

- *The unknown are Her eggs and sperm combining together causing a combustion*

- *Creating an explosion, The Big Bang*

- *For the Big Bang is in Her womb*

- *For the Big Bang is in the multiverse*

- *For when the eggs and sperm combings together it causes a spark*

- *And that spark forms into a heart*

- *As the stars explode giving birth to many stars and many suns*

- *For we are the stars and sun that she created in her womb*

- *How can I stop my mind from contemplating about this*

- *Contemplating about Mother of a Nation, Queen Goddess, Nubian Flower, Sweetness, Love-ness, Beauty-ness...*

- *She stands tall with her hands in the heavens wrapped in the light of Ra*

- *Fellows, gentlemen we have to put are egos aside on this one*

- *And just hear me out on this one*

- *Because of the 2012 procession and mother earth & Her Transformation*

- *Before there was Wiseman we had Wise Woman*

- *Before there was Wise Emperors we had Wise Empresses*

- *Before there was Wise Gods we had Wise Goddess*

- *For it was the Queens that crowned the Kings way back in the days*

- *Way way back in the days on TaMaRe, nowadays called Egypt*

- *Her Wisdom is glorious, and never fades away*

- *She goes on and about seeking those who are worthy of her*

- *For She is the sacred and holy place of divine creation*

- *Her womb of Triple Divine Darkness is a direct reflection of the multi-verse where the whole of creation was created*

- *Her rule of creation by the ten spheres of manifestation, Nubian Goddess are the only ones capable to bring forth life*

- *For the very true beginning of her is the desire for discipline, then it forms into Love*

- *And for Her Love is the keeping of her universal law*

- *And for the keeping of Her universal law is to become near to her*

- *As for wisdom what she is and how she comes about*

- *I can only tell you one thing and that is to look up into the multiverse for her wisdom is unlimited*

- *Look into yourself, For her wisdom is infinite*

- *How can I stop my mind form contemplating*

- *Contemplating about Mother of a Nation, Queen Goddess, Nubian Flower Sweetness, Love-ness... Mother Wise.*

Clouds of Ecstasy

- *Ecstasy: An exhilarated trancelike desirable condition or a state of exalted delightful bliss, An overwhelming pleasure, joy-able sensation, a state of mind, Heaven on earth, also known as cloud nine*

- *You put me on Cloud Ecstasy every time I be feelin your innerG*

- *Even the very first day we talk on the phone that same night I went to a mental paradise with you and not even know you*

- *And sense that day we have been on the phone for 20 straight more days*

- *Having conversation that stimulate our mental connection*

- *On both ends of our phone our emotion is rising to that one specific zone*

- *That Cloud 9!!!*

- *That Cloud Ecstasy!!!*

- *Exchanging poetry late nights on the phone*

- *Listening to each other vibration and tones*

- *You send chills up my back bones with that laugh of yours*

- *That one specific laugh that you laugh when we be on Cloud Ecstasy*

- *Yea... Real sexy*

- *I can't wait for the day you come down*

- *Together we stand rising to the mental plane*

- *Making sweet love to each other's mind*

- *Enjoying that ride on Cloud 9*

- *Enjoying that ride on Cloud Ecstasy*

- *You see, I can't wait till that day comes when we can look into each other eyes and we both will be mesmerize on that natural high*

- *We will be like two magnets*

- *Always attracted towards each other and never letting go*

- *For I am God's angel*

- *I am that perfect stranger that you long for*

- *To treat you the way you want to be treated*

- *Like a Nubian Goddess*

- *I will take you into my hands and lift you up into the Heavens*

- *And gently place you on Cloud Ecstasy*

- *Only if you knew what your feelings do to me*

- *And don't worry about these clouds being dissipated*
  cause these clouds here will never be faded

- *So let's lay down on Cloud 9 and look into the universe at the stars*

- *Enjoying the beautiful view*

- *Man I am so high riding on Cloud 9*

- *Cause you know you be my dime and sunshine*

- *Let me put this pen down*

- *I'll wait for the day you come down*

- *Then we can sip on some fine wine*

- *On Cloud 9*

- *Cloud Ecstasy*

- *Yea… Real Sexy*

Can I Get To Know You?

- *I see you with my physical eyes, but then again do I*

- *What you see of me, my flesh is nothing more than a space suit I am wearing out here in this womb-averse protecting what's more valuable within*

- *I stand in front of you looking into our big brown eyes*

- *Trying to get to a place where no one have reach not*

- *A place where not many will over-stand*

- *However when I see you it's just an illusion to the eye and the mind.*

- *For our bodies is made up of minute particles from the ground*

- *So what comes from the ground, is it an illusion*

- *Man my mind is going crazy*

- *My mind is going crazy thinking about this world of delusion*

- *Thinking about this world of delusion has my mind going round and round like a merry-go-round*

- *For if you are an illusion then does it mean that this world we are living in is not real*

- *Or is it because we are both earthbound*

- *If our flesh is not the real I nor the real you then how can I get to know you?*

- *Would it be a waste of my InnerG and would it be in vain to what to feel you?*

- *Would it be worthless to what to Love you?*

- *So please tell me how can I get to know you, if what I see is nothing more but just atoms form beneath my feet and I underneath yours*

- *I don't know, but I will over stand*

- *So let's go ahead and expand our minds beyond our likes & dis-likes*

- *Expand our minds beyond our feelings of attraction*

- *If not there will always be an reaction to that*

- *A reaction to our cause and effect, isn't it*

- *An attraction from my eyes to yours stimulating the reaction, stimulating the reaction*

- *The reaction is your magnetic attraction filling my body with electricity from your InnerG*

- *You see by now you should know that you have a magnetic pull, Pulling all eyes in sight of you*

- *You have some attracting magnetic powers of some sort, that is pulling my emotion and desires & Igniting my center fire*

- *Now if I identify with these feelings a little too much then I will fall in this materialistic realm*

- *Making it impossible for me to turn my body into a sham so I can go off to the next realm*

- *How can I get to know you without any fears of me putting to many emotions into you*

- *Tell me?*

- *Tell me how can I get to know you without setting myself up in this world of delusion*

- *So what is your solution in me getting to know you*

- *You see I know the way to you heart*

- *And you know my tone is like playing Mozart in your ears*

- *Girl how can I get to know you if what I see is the egoism*

- *An illusion of your physical body*

- *The I-ness and the my-ness which is not the real you*

- *Now that I am blind how can I get to know you or see you if everything I see is an illusion*

- *Now I would like to know from you is your spirit is as beautiful as your Birthday suit?*

- *Is it?*

- *That is my question to you*

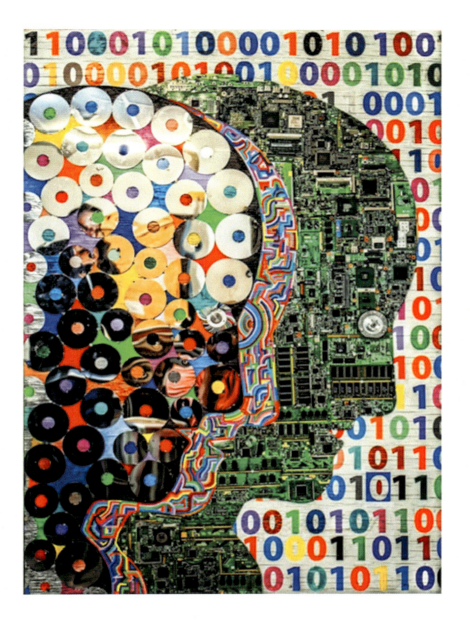

Just Wondering

- *I wonder how it will be when she finds out that I am her King*

- *Wondering on all the possibility on what it will be like*

- *What it will be when we sit down and elevate our spirits*

- *Wondering how high we will get off that natural high*

- *That high off each other's presence*

- *I wonder how her reaction will be when she finds out the vowel I*
- *Made to myself before we met*
- *I wonder what she will think about, me seeing myself in her*
- *Me being her God as she's my Goddess*
- *I'll wonder how it will feel like*
- *We'll just worship each other to help up lift one another*
- *That's how I imagine it would be*

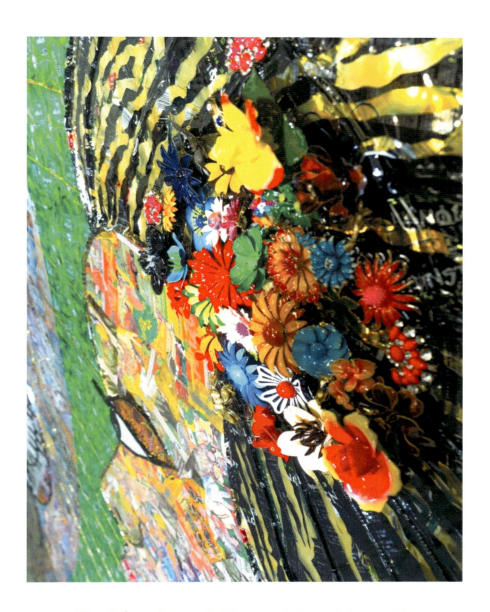

To The One I Have Not Meet Yet

- *Pt. I*

- *This is to that one Nubian Goddess I have not meet yet*

- *She makes me feel Her sweetness*

- *Her kindness*

- *Her niceness*

- *Her melodious sound as they vibrate in my ears*

- *Her attentiveness to hear my vibration and tones*

- *Her friendliness to make time, when she knows she has no time*

- *Her agreeableness*

- *Her beloved InnerG*

- *Her Inner InnerG*

- *Her Chi InnerG*

- *Man it feels so Heavenly*

- *Her precious Love feels so Heavenly*

- *Her pleasant thoughts*

- *Her delicate sound*

- *Her mellowness*

- *Her gentleness*

- *Soft and compassionate she is*

- *Yea… Just the way I like her*

- *How can one know so mush and feel so much about that Nubian Goddess they have not met yet*

- *I have no idea*

- *But Her energy is felt all within my soul*

- *Her InnerG is felt all within my whole entire being*

- *At times I feel as thou she is around me*

- *Maybe because she may be the air that I breathe*

- *That's why she is one with me*

- *Her Love*

- *Her tenderness is felt*

- *Her heart beat is felt*

- *Her InnerG-In-motion are felt*

  - *Her cheerfulness*

  - *Her silliness at times*

- *Man… Her being is so delightful*

- *Her InnerG is so beautiful*

- *This is to that one Nubian Goddess I haven't met yet.*

Pt. II

- *Half my lifetime I've waited for that one special person
  that person that I've created in my mind*

- *In every way, form and fashion she would be able to make me feel fine*

- *Intertwined with both our minds we would be as one.*

- *I've prayed to the source innerG numerous of times
  that it would send you my way and it did*

- *Identifying if you were the one was easy*

- *It was that late night on the beach when it was feeling real cool and breezy*

- *Me holding your hands I felt all your InnerG*

- *You see, the way you make me feel is in words that I've written before*

- *Yes!!! Your right, the feeling is all familiar*

- *Just as I am familiar to you*

- *You are as familiar to me*

- *A manifestation in my mind, He has brought you to me*

- *The first time we penetrated eyes I was like*

- *"Yeah!!! I'm feeling her InnerG"*

- *So I share myself with you*

- *I share my being with you*

- *My intimate self longs for you*

- *To the one I have not met yet*

- *I am happy and gland to say*

- *"I have finally met you"*

- *I will introduce myself to you as Amon-Ra*

- *Yes!!! Intimate we are*

Dove in the Sky

- *Brought to me like a Dove from the sky*

- *Automatically this Dove becomes Queen Goddess*

- *Black Woman*

- *Nubian Flower*

- *Mother Earth*

- *Queen Mother of the Universe*

- *To uplift this Queen, is to uplift the world*

- *Full sight of her in heaven without restraint*

- *Heavenly paradise lies at the feet of this Queen*

- *This Goddess may be heaven on earth*

- *Came all in black as pure as her mind*

- *Black as her womb in front of her spine*

- *She is divine*

- *Born of heavenly seed*

- *In perfect beauty did not first perceive*

- *Her skin*

- *Her face a golden completion*

- *Oh… What a beautiful sight*

- *She is the Moon that gives out the light*

- *I wake, she fled, and brought back my night*

- *I can go on and on about this Goddess*

- *But why*

- *Why!!!*

- *When I know sooner or later this Dove will fly, fly away*

Infusion

- We infuse each other's energy with our mental waves
  our conversations and intriguing vibration

- Knowing that our affection would be strong towards each other

- And at times we ask ourselves is this going to last forever

- Compelled in sharing our most intimate thoughts as we
  hear the words flow out of our mental realm

- We both speak forth our every existence to come meet on this realm

- Our reality is now formed

- Waiting for her to come from the west

- Looking at how bright she is, as the sunset

- *Sitting on my throne patiently waiting, for I am the deity Set*

   - *And the pen goes down, fast forward in time*

      - *Substance will be found*

Beautiful Tantra

- *I don't see nothing wrong with a little bump and grind.*

- *And everywhere that I go I can see it in her eyes.*

- *And everywhere that I go I can see it in her eyes.*

- *What is it that you see in her eyes?*

- *Nothing but high sexual InnerG*

- *Knowin she wants to feel me*

- *Knowin she wants to sex me*

- *Who she think she's foolin*

- *Not me*

- *You see I just be playing a fool*

- *Even thou I just what to rule the higher self in me*

- *So please listen to me baby*

- *Even thou I be telling you lets go with the flow*

- *However I went against the flow*

- *Unintentionally*

- *Holding myself back away from you*

- *Knowing it would make you want me even more and more*

- *Intriguing your mind far beyond comprehension*

- *Far beyond our comprehension of our own sexual desires*

- *We wanting to feel the sensation of each other's skin that we so long admire*

- *So therefore I desire you*

- *As I picture and imagine the best part of your body, while you do the same thing in your mind*

- *For me it is those Eyes*

- *Those full Beautiful illustrious lips*

- *And those sexy ass thighs*

- *As you keep these thoughts mesmerize in your mind of me sexing you and you sexing me*

- *It just makes me want to get closer and closer in between those thighs*

- *Never be mention or no need to mention with words of utterance*

- *Because we can exchange each other sexual InnerG with our eyes*

- *Exchange it with our mental wave link*

- *Cause our minds in sync*

- *I come to realize there's no need for me to deprive myself of the warm heat and the sweet Heavenly Nectars that are in between those thighs that you long to provide*

- *So let's meet in between the sheets*

- *Where we can feel each other's heart beat*

- *As our body collide*

- *Like the medical helix trolling around*

- *We can combine ourselves just to do the bump and grind*

- *So why waste time*

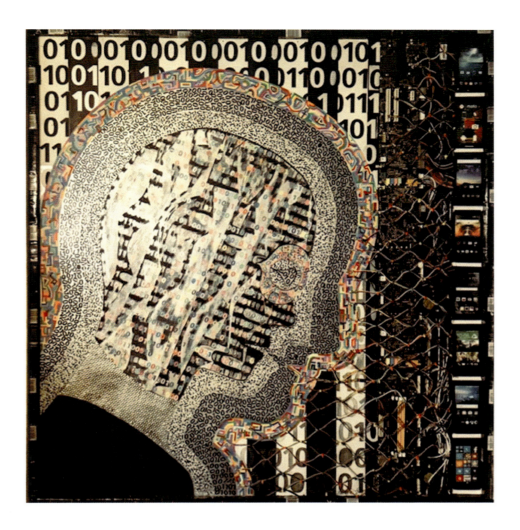

Note To Inner Self

When we surrender our Love and heart we will be enabled once again to regain the use of our 3rd eye. Once we get our desires and wants under control we will be the ruler of the body, instead of the body ruling us. At this point the body is no longer in need and we will have become a supreme being. By regaining that supreme stature we then become that Divine Being that we were meant to be. That's why it is said that we can be able to leave our physical body and rise our self-up. We will no longer need the physical body and this material world. Only with positive prayer/affirmation, positive meditation, proper exercise, proper diet, cheerfulness, being giving, and patience we can be able to become our divine self.

Intoxicated Love Pt. I

- *The divine essence through your eyes is the way to heaven.*

- *Without your Love, the all would be incomplete and feeling your Love is what makes me whole*

- *Your innerG gets me high when I think of you, my spirit flies when I am next to you*

- *Just listening to you talk about your views of life and your philosophies is a sure thing that we will always have something to talk about.*

- *So I will always Injoy myself with u. And I will always be in LOVE with u and your presence*

- *Let it be written, let it be done, it is done, in good faith, so be it.*

This Little Light of Mine

(Chorus)

- *This little light of mine, I'm going to let it shine*

- *This little light of mine, I'm going to let it shine*

- *Let it shine, let it shine, let it shine*

- *Everywhere that I go, I'm going to let it shine*

- *Everywhere that I go, I'm going to let it shine*

- *Let it shine, let it shine, let it shine*

- *This little light of mine that rest right here on my chest*

- *I will let it shine within my whole inner being*

- *My whole solar within*

- *What gives me life within Amon Ra the hidden one within*

- *We as poets being able to stand here in front of this mic is nothing more but just being Godlike*

- *Just like how Gods spoke the word and created the sun*

- *We spite fire that ignites our center fire*

- *Maybe we'll say the right things to ignite your center fire*

- *Remember the sun is within us*

- *This little light of mine is Ra*

- *Like raw vegetables a nourishment to your soul*

- *For the soul is the light*

- *Just like how Horus said or Yashu'a or Jesus said, all one in the same*

- *Just like how he said in Matthew 6:22 and again in Luke 11:34 "The light of the body is the eye, and when that eye is single our body is also full of light but when that eye is evil and closed our body is also filled with darkness"*

- *And again in that good ghost-spell, I mean that gospel of John1:1-5 "In the beginning was the word and the word was with God (Source InnerG), and the word (Om) was God. The same was in the beginning with (Source InnerG) God. All things were made by Source InnerG and without it was not anything made that was made. In Source InnerG was life, and life was the light of man. And the light shined in the darkness and the darkness comprehended it not."*

- *And this is why we were thought (Thoth) this song as a young one in church*

- *I never knew the meaning of what it was worth*

- *Now that my 3rd eye is open, I have a better over standing of this little light of mine.*

(Chorus)

- *This little light of mine, I'm going to let it shine*

- *This little light of mine, I'm going to let it shine*

- *Let it shine, let it shine, let it shine*

- *Everywhere that I go, I'm going to let it shine*

- *Everywhere that I go, I'm going to let it shine*

- *Let it shine, let it shine, let it shine*

- *This little light of mine is the light of my universe*

- *For it is my sustainer within I*

- *We are the light of the world*

- *For the light of the body is the eye, the eye Ra*

- *Our whole body is full of light because we are the whole light beings*

- *Because Source InnerG & our ancestors dwell within*

- *All colors of the chakras I try my BES to vibrate*

- *Elevate my mind then I begin to cultivate this little light of mine.*

- *For this light has grown into a bigger light*

- *Which has allowed me to find my true passion in life*

- *And no it is not the true passion of Christ*

- *It is by the way of the true passion in I, Spoken Word*

- *By way of HuHi, Thoth, Tehuti, my words becomes flesh*

- *By way of HuHi, Thoth, Tehuti my words is felt*

- *Feelin the Chi that they bring into me, crown chakra wide open*

- *Spirit Guide descend*

- *Chi Going down my spine and back up my kundalini*

- *Feelin the true essence of a natural high*

- *Gettin high @ first it was with any substance need be*

- *Whether it be the weed the Gin, or the Hennessey*

- *Now it be that Chi that lay deep within Thee*

- *That Eye, that light*

- *This little light of mine shines within and outside of me*

- *Ra is the light that shines within in every man and womb-men*

- *And until then we need to stop lookin for this higher force or this higher being outside of we and look within thee*

- *Cause the light of the body is that eye*

- *The eye of Ra*

- *For Allah is in me*

- *Jah is in I*

- *For the source innerG is in we*

- *And if you don't believe me read Psalms 83*

- *And until then we will not be able to bring forth our true divinity so all to see*

- *Tap into our solar so we can fulfill our true destiny*

- *Being thought (Thoth) this song as a young one in church I never knew the meaning of what it was worth*

- *Now that my 3rd eye is open*

- *I have a better over standing of this little light of mine*

- *So now I sing it loud and proud*

(Chorus)

- *This little light of mine, I'm going to let it shine*

- *This little light of mine, I'm going to let it shine*

- *Let it shine, let it shine, let it shine*

- *Everywhere that I go, I'm going to let it shine*

- *Everywhere that I go, I'm going to let it shine*

- *Let it shine, let it shine, let it shine*

Intoxicated Love Pt. II

- *I wake up from out of my sleep to find ways on how
  I can have u melt in the palm of my hands.*

- *I've waited and search for the one that would allow me this act.*

- *So I sit listening to love songs and write about how we would soak and bath
  in each other's emotions that we will create in our own heavens of elevation.*

- *Bringing forth to life with our mental connection and
  with words sound power. Elevation!!!!*

- *Why not Love each other even though we have not meet yet*

- *That's the beautiful thing about spirit*

- *Cause our spirit attracted one another*

  - *Our Spirits are meet to Love*

    - *Love Compassionately*

      - *Unconditional Love*

        - *Delicately Love*

        - *Gracefully Love*

        - *Exquisitely Love*

      - *That real Love, Love*

        - *That Elegant Love*

        - *Charming Love*

        - *Seductively Love*

        - *Tastefully Love*

        - *Magnificent Love*

  - *That… That… Divine Universal One Love*

- *So let's go to a place where our spirit over-stands this Love.*

  - *The Love for that God, & Goddess within us*

    - *Pass cloud 9 and pass cloud ecstasy*

  - *A place where the sky's open up to our prayers*

- *Wanting to stay in that place and over indulge on that sensation*

  - *Our intoxication for one another*

  - *Intoxicated off that Divine Love*

- *Old ancient spirits we are*

- *So let's continue to manifest what we always wanted.*

- *One another*

- *Let it be done*

- *It is Done*

- *In good faith*

- *So Be It*

Spirit Guide

Be my mind 🧠 & in my thinking
Be my 👁 & in my vision
Be my ears & in my hearing
Be my mouth & in my speaking
Be my heart 💜 & in my overstanding
Be my hands 🤲 & in my doing
Be my solar 🔥 & in my reaction
Be my feet 👣 & my path
Spirit guide be in all that I do
Help me to be you 🙏👳🙏
Amen 😈
🤭sorry wrong emoji 😇
😜🤪😜
I can't help my silly 🙃 side

Cousin

- *Writing this poem for you*

- *Thinking this would be an easy task for me*

- *But it wasn't*

- *Every night I cry myself to sleep as my mind sings sad songs*

- *Totally forgetting what it takes to write a poem*

- *Deep inner emotions about your death begin to arise
  more and more, which made it difficult*

- *This sudden tragedy of you being gone is a heavy blow to the family*

- *It's like a deep laceration to the side that needs stitches*

- *And in time the wounds will heal*

- *Family is one of the main things you and I always talked about*

- *Having conversations about how happy you were on that very last day*

- *And on that Sunday was the day that you made your rounds*

- *Stopping by family members houses that was closes by just to say Hi*

- *Even calling those afar just to say I love*

- *So you and I continued to have conversations
  on how closer our family needed to be*

- *You asking me, why is it that families always
  gather together at weddings or funerals*

- *Never in a million years I would have thought that seeing
  you drive away would be the last time seeing you alive*

- *Well Gardy we are all here*

- *I know there is a higher meaning to your sudden departure*

  - *You have brought us all here together*

- *I am sorry that it is under these circumstance that we all gather together*

  - *So I pray to the ancestors that they show us the higher meaning behind your sudden departure*

- *On a positive note cousin, we will truly miss you, everything about you*

  - *I will miss you knocking on my window at odd times at night just to stop by to tell me that you love me.*

- *You have affected the lives of so many people in so many ways*

  - *I know that your spirit is in a better place*

    - *You will continue to live on*

  - *Through your Arch Angels Michel & Gabriel*

  - *Let your spirit return home to source InnerG and may our ancestors bless your soul*

    - *I miss you & Love you man.*

R.I.P Gardy Louissaint

01/02/82 – 05/19/13

Autobiography

Amon Ra Nabmare is a spoken word artist from South Florida. He has been writing poetry for 16 years, and has been preforming at open Mic, & spoken word events. Amon Ra has set out to motivate and inspire people with his timeless poems from his life experience.

Facebook: Amon Ra Nebmare

Instagram: @Nomadicgems.5

All abstract art work in this book is done by the International & National awards winning artist Duken Delpe

Facebook: Duke of art

Instagram: Duken_delpe_bluedaddy_maker

Printed in the United States
By Bookmasters